# BINOCULARS

**ALSO BY DOUGLAS LAWDER**

*Trolling*
Little, Brown and Company

# BINOCULARS

## DOUGLAS LAWDER

NFSPS PRESS
ROCHESTER HILLS MI

## ACKNOWLEDGMENTS

Many of these poems have appeared or will appear in *Atlanta Review*, *The Bellingham Review*, *Caesura*, *Cumberland Poetry Review*, *Gulf Coast*, *Louisiana Literature*, *Manhattan Poetry Review*, *National Forum*, *Poetry Review* (Poetry Society of America), *The Runner* and *Southern Poetry Review*.

The author is grateful to the Corporation of Yaddo, the MacDowell Colony, the Wurlitzer Foundation, the Karolyi Foundation, and the Edna St. Vincent Millay Colony for time and occasion for the writing of these poems; to the Colorado Council on the Arts for support in the development of this collection; and to Renée Ruderman for her help and encouragement.

*Book Design*   Lee Ballentine
*Cover Design*   Todd Anderson
*Photography*   Standish Lawder
*Manufacturing Coordination*   Jennifer MacGregor
*Project Coordination*   Margo LaGattuta

Library of Congress cataloging-in-publication data is available for this title.

This publication is the 2000 winner of the National Federation of State Poetry Societies Stevens Poetry Manuscript Competition. Publication does not constitute endorsement in ideas or language by the NFSPS. Rather, it specifically endorses the idea of freedom of speech on the part of the poet, and of the autonomy of the judge who selected the winning manuscript, principles we believe to be important for all literary competitions. While a poem may not reflect the tastes of some of our membership, we believe strongly that poets must remain uncensored.

This competition is an annual competition with a deadline of October 15th. Complete rules and information on the purchase of past publications may be obtained by contacting Amy Zook, NFSPS Stevens Poetry Manuscript Chairman, 3520 St. Rd 56, Mechanicsburg OH 43044.

*Published by*
NFSPS Press
3128 Walton Blvd P.M.B. 186
Rochester Hills MI 48309

Once again, for my children

.

.

.

BINOCULARS

The land is like poetry; it is inexplicably coherent,
it is transcendent in its meaning, and it has the power
to elevate a consideration of human life.
*Barry Lopez*

# Contents

4 ▦ *Duplicate moon*

# Foreword

I chose *Binoculars* to be the First Place manuscript for several reasons. This is the work of a mature poet who understands the power of language to renew not only the writer's spirit but also the reader's. The author of *Binoculars*, as the title would suggest, sees life as a close observer, one who can focus on details so acutely that the sharpness of vision alone can bring us to tears. The author uses language precisely, especially with strong verbs, as if the words themselves have been studied through binoculars.

The real success of this manuscript, however, seems to me to be how the author observes through both ends of the binoculars: we receive the long view as well as the close-up. In "Swimming Before Sleep," for example, the author ends the poem by placing a particular experience into a larger vision:

> Down below a bubbling sound like
> water in the throat and the bulk
> of a submerged houseboat grunts
> as it settles again in silt.
> Sleep is, I think, a serum, a way
> of defending ourselves from sleep,
> that final sinking, that
> treading on a half-rotten board
> and breaking through.

These are poems to read aloud, as well. The author has an exceptional sense of rhythm and sound, qualities I find lacking in much of the poetry I read. The rhythm is not imposed; it grows from the sounds of the words, an attention to the duration of syllables as well as their percussion. The imagery triggers all of the senses and the author's use of internal rhyme enhances the power of the images.

All of these qualities come together to give this author a powerful voice. But that's not all, and that alone probably would not have made this the winning manuscript. This is a unified collection of poems organized into four sections held together by the author's voice and a cluster of images and themes. In many ways, the book resembles a symphony with water as a major motif.

*Kenneth W. Brewer*
*teaches Creative Writing*
*and is Director of Graduate*
*Studies in English at*
*Utah State University*

# 1

## Looking to Survive

# Triangulations

Noon and from this crooked wing of the library
we seem to lurch like a ship
off course across the fogged campus
and the faint boom of rain
pebbles the roof and people
sober as fish move past windows
running with water. Well, I think,
we try to chart, to
triangulate our way.

All afternoon rain keeps falling.
Umbrellas like gaudy mushrooms bloom
on the library steps. All day it's
research we've been after going down
deeper and deeper, rolling up what's known
into a ball. Perhaps the trick's to shape
facts right so they won't roll back on the shaper,
to steer clear of what's uncharted.

In the evening lightning zig-zags down
as if stitching earth and sky together.
From this window I see a bright shot chip
the roof. A tail of light snakes and jumps
like St. Elmo's fire and dunks
in the gutter. Now lights in the library dim
to a bathysphere's deep sea probing.
Then some thing like a singed cloth,
like a piece of wetfire smoking flares up
way beyond a color that's ever been seen before,
like foxfire floating,
a dead star falling,
like what might shoot up once in the brain
and then be gone.

2

# Islands

*What absorbs me in these birds... is how adroitly
each (one) joins the larger flock or departs from it.
And how each bird while it is a part of the flock
seems part of something larger than itself. Another
animal.* Barry Lopez, *Arctic Dreams*

Day and night you hold
in your head the word
*island, island* and think of
water spreading out on all sides,
how it flows loosely together
and of what keeps this island together:
roots that interlock like hands,
their intricate underground meshing.

In the woods in
a sudden clearing
there's a dis-
assembled skeleton,
its arpeggio of bones,
scattered teeth all
with their own white shape,
the heavy curl and smooth
lathing like shells flung up
from the sea's floor.

Tonight stars are strewn
so clearly across the sky it seems
as if they had once all fit together.
From inside,
a descanting flute, a voice
braid themselves
into one ribbon of light.

Day and night you hold
in your head the word
*island, island*
and come to know
how all things must be
separate coming together.

*Ossabaw Island, Georgia*

# Sand and Snow

It's poised mid-
way between Alpine meadows
and where, below, the desert wind's
always at work reshaping sand,
a place cupped in a mountain tensed
between snow and sand and which
like the first garden or where ever
such loveliness gathers
it's at great cost.

You come down-mountain
and hear the river's stone songs
in the fast run-off of snow.
In town scraps of valley mist
dampen down smoke of piñon burning
that oldest smell of man.
Then April's rain begins to thin out blood
that's soaked this valley:
blond scalps hung out to dry,
Indians blasted from adobe churches.
There are killer dogs that lope in gangs.
They know how red the earth beneath them is.

But when the misted air clears
bright as a shout and the earth steams thick
and white as if casting out its bones,
millions of lemony flames--sun-struck pollen--
explode and hang in the air, bob
on thermals above the river's gorge, go
floating up-mountain
abundant and brilliant as snow flake or silica
to where sacred Blue Lake's cupped like an eye.

*Taos, New Mexico*

5

# Binoculars

*That this eye not be folly's loophole*
*But giver of due regard.*  Richard Wilbur

For brother Standish, film maker

You sent them to me twenty years ago.
Here's some myth or history still
preserved in their angled Corridors:
a twisted scarf of snow wind-
lifted above the timberline, then,
down valley an elk herd
browsing under bunched trees.
Lucy sails her cat boat over Mirror Lake,
those splashed drops of water
like contact lenses on her shoulder.

Always at their windows,
trying to get the world into focus,
like a filmstrip that loops and loops again, eyes
are the small hard-jellied brains hooked
on always looking.

Here as in a kind of preserve,
this late 19th century estate, we're
all voyeurs. In the Tower Room banked
behind a heavy slab of glass I'm
in quarantine. A half mile away where
the sward ends at a splashing fountain
tourists gawk at the Tudor mansion.
I dial the lenses into focus
and someone jumps into sight.
He has a camera for a face.
When he gets this picture back
there'll be a dim figure caught
at the window looking back, a creature,
his eyes on black stalks staring,
looking to survive
and then might ask: how
to see the seer
from what's perceived?

*Yaddo, Saratoga Springs, N.Y.*

# Taking Shape

Still snarled in the dark net of sleep.
To climb from the chaos of another's dream,
I run blind in the pre-dawn snow
down a valley made by plows
throwing up snow all night.
Like blurred fingerprints
my running tracks wane
then ghost out.

But when the sun comes up
and with this first snow
a kind of light
that's never been inside before
comes through windows.
Off of miles of fields outside
snow shine pours through pure as paper
and there's a line
of icicles hanging from the roof
—bright possibilities—like new nails.
On the back porch each running shoe stands
bent to a form
holding its own
true shape of the foot.

Now walls seem to fall away,
the ceiling rising to a dome
and these typewriter keys
are rounded in white and waiting
for what's yet to be done.

8

# Touch

In this cab on 5th Ave.
a woman's left her glove,
doe or moleskin, an expensive scent
of both pink and black
and I think of her high
above the city touch-
ing flame to candlesticks,
fingers fixed with stone, the ring
of cut glass Baccarat
before the gossip of politics and art.

And you in your loft beginning to quarry the night,
finessing the stone you love
even before the shape you make it become.
Your nicked fingers, burr of thumb callus,
smashed knuckle joint
wheedle from the fired grain,
make it comply to your hand
—this up-turned, battered hand—
doppelgänger of your own:
articulated pride,
and the way it informs down to the bone
what touch is.

# Lake Light

You wake with wet-light spill-
ing from limbs—this lake shimmer
filling the room, the ceiling water-
rippled, walls of shine.

The kitchen's a chamber of light:
the coffee pot struck with a watery gong,
bright clatter of spoons,
light shaking through the faucet's flow
—a flame in sunshine,
cellophane burning.

The broad lake's squared
to the living room mirror, now
made perfectly round and deep
as a well by the glass-top table.

It's a dream of watery light descending,
of evening's long reach:
slow flutter of shine on the far wall
like water thinning and thinning.
A shiver of doused light.
A splashing through shallows down
the widening circles of sleep.

# Balances, A Lake Journal

Its aggregate needles of ice,
   slow creak of their growing,
   stitch upon stitch
   until ice is an eye-shaped rock
   rolled into the lake—a locked vault
   except at forty feet below:
   nerve tick,
   slight pulse of spring,
   webbing and tightening
   a clock running down.
   At night the lake's
   a blind, unblinking eye,
   gong-round.

---

Break up starts with pistol shots.
   Garage-sized ice chunks ride up on shore.
   Others topple with the crash of a heaved-over piano,
   giving back to water what
   ice held of it all winter
   —its marbled greens and blues—
   what was kept in escrow. Silence,
   a caesura as if for thought.
   Frost smoke. Tickings.
Then the lake seems to tip again:
   a winking of small gears,
   bright pieces of a broken clock
   and tons of costume jewelry
   sliding up, sluicing on the shore.
   Night's a chiming of glass on glass
   resounding off storm windows.

---

Summer lake water brimming,
    its muscled, undulant motion
    needled with sun fleck until
    a curtain of rain carries over the lake.
    All afternoon its hiss and ping
    of coupling where water meeting water's
    the sound of slant rhyme falling into evening,
    then a fine drizzle modulates to plain song.

————————

There's a time in fall when the earth pauses
    on a threshold;
    it's a key holding the tumblers of a lock just so,
    right before the weighted door swings to.
    Now more than ever the world bears watching:
    a waterbird flies over the lake.
    Each balanced wing-flick touches water,
    dimples a double row of shallow pools.
    They look like a serial set of eyes, as

I fit a matching lens of storm windows over each window.
    They take and hold lake light then give it back again.
    There's a balance to this as with the word *eye*–
    a way of bearing witness to the world so that it might
        bear witness back:
    The day's trapped breath is also held for awhile between glass,
    as will the lake when it caps the last of the year's breath
    under a thin lens of ice before the full weight of it
    fills the lake's socket up.

# 2

**With a mind to what the body knows**

# Ceremony on Fish Lake

For Charlotte

Dawn and the lake's slick
as rubbed rock with a white
over-inscription of mist.
Five in a boat. It *Vs* to dead-
center and stops where they sit
and wait for more light.
Like a series of eyes
the water's row holes
close over.

*Now,* she says and turns
the jar over.
Except for the ting
of a dental filling, small
rattle, knock
of arthritic knuckle bone,
ashes slide out like a sigh,
water at first re-
fusing to take them in: a
curved film the shape
of an arm thrown back in sleep,
a bent question mark clots
on the lid of the lake.
Then a silver scar that just
pulls apart spreading out
thin as a caul
and with the sun rising up
on the lake their mother's
final loss of shape's a
cloud, thin breath of smoke
and then like that of water.

# Cold Snap

*What else must have Noah seen?*

Rain flooded through meadows,
washed into the woods, fog and more
rain until one cold night snap froze
water clear down to the ground on which
we knelt and saw the green fields preserved,
each blade of grass and ribbed fern
pressed into place, magnified pebbles.
Then we flew over the earth on skates
suspended from the world's weight.
Entering the woods were other rooms:
underfoot a lacquered frieze of branches,
twigs holding still-green leaves,
boulders napped with lichen tumbled
from a collapsed stone wall,
bracelets of barbed wire.

At twilight the flattened sun
spread a red fire across the ice
which held the small flames
of skate-shaved ice and when we saw
first the fur, then the head
of a calf, its chin resting on
a doubled-up knee, its goggle-
eyed look through ice as if
pickled in a jar
we couldn't stop from looking.
Our little lungs puffed out
puzzling white balloons
in cold clarity
of what not breathing is.

# After Mowing: Land and Water

There's an after-roar in the ears
as what we'd hear in the whorls of a shell
and the lawn's now smooth as suede,
as the contiguous lake where a fleet
of cut grass patrols.
A scarf of blue smoke in the air.
The mower cools in the shed and leaf shade's
nicely pronounced on the clipped lawn.
The mashed and minted scent of grass
drifts over the lake.

Dozing on the dock we're free
for awhile from land,
from the gravity of growing grass
where water offers its own solution:
beginning its metronome knock of waves,
that begins to implicate our sleep
from where down below
water rattles shells and lake stones,
nudging them over and back
easy as breathing.

# The Policy

Sometimes I wake in the dead of night
and the lake's reddened with fire again,
the crack of a joist crashing through club-
bing the kitchen sink, the stairs giving way
falling into the closet's pile of burning
winter coats, the tropical smell
of coffee, tea and cloves forged
into blackened lumps, my right hand
on fire, the zig-zag stitch of flame up
Laura's nightgown as we race for the lake
and then red sirens of fire trucks sear-
ing the night adding red to red over what
little's left of the house where later
the whole mess and debris was
buried and bulldozed flat.

Though this morning the sun comes up
warming these walls that smell of fresh
plaster and paint and a long window's
been cut that shows a sweep of the lake
shore we'd never seen before from inside,
sometimes on damp evenings a mephitic stench
will make its claim seeping up
from under the house into the newly cut
hardwood floors and taint what's just
been freshly starched and varnished
and which the agent tells me
can't be covered.

# Winter Fever

Seen through doubled glass two deer
come back from the brook
where they've sucked up icy water.
Their ears curve to the tiniest forest's snap.
Breathing thick vapor back to the chill air
they leap the fence, bound over snow flushed red,
climb to a high sanctuary of sleep
thicketed just inside the timber line
where the day's last light touches down.

Wincing from snowshine we labor wheezing up to bed,
to sheets and a white quilt heaped
like mounds of soiled snow.
The vaporizer fills the room
with a specious vernal scent.
Its clacking sound seems all night
the soul's machinery sprocketing down
fevered loops of sleep and into dreams
of stuttering half-light.

# Reading Fiction at 3 AM

I knew the woods outside:
small eyes of the hot rain
hanging everywhere, the ground
soft as wet bread and the clear-
ing dank as a mouth.
But just after a night
traveler's car lights
swept through the room,
that noise like a claw
scraped against glass,
a red sound of some-
thing small and furred, talon-
gashed that pulsed and stopped
and spurted again like blood
in the beaded, unblinking night
and just as quickly stopped.
I got up as if waking from
someone else's dream, walked
through this room I
thought I knew, rapped
the mantle for proof of its soundness,
passed my hand under lamplight
to see for sure its flesh wrapped
solid around each fingerbone,
stood listening with a mind
to what the body knows.

# Vista, Twilight

Scent of perfume in the elevator
and last night's greenwood smokes in the fireplace
and from the 14th floor sun fades from the scaled
    glaciers on Long's Peak
and far below lights of other lives click on
and this sip of whiskey is its own past
and the heirloom clock ticks its
*what was  what was  what was.*

# Waiting for Sleep

*A blanker whiteness of benighted snow*  Robert Frost

In this valley a spell
of leucophobia:
dreaming of glaciers on the divide,
of mountain meadows at 14,000 feet
where snow's always falling
darklighting days
so there's no land, no sky, snow
building laminate layers
bonded by hoar frost and pingo
cushioned killer drifts riding up to 40 feet
beguiling by what can't be seen or known—
terra incognita,
Atlantis of one's dreams,
of late-night imaginings.

# Swimming before Sleep

*With water he defends himself from water.*
*The drowning sea*
*Is all he has between himself and drowning.*
Robert Francis

Sun down. Some
after glow off the lake.
A reluctance to snap
lights on. I walk by braille
through darkening rooms of the house
inviting night in. Then the lake
shimmers on windows, some watery stars
sway in the mirror.

The curled fingers of water
are hollow sounds under the dock.
I imagine the heavy carp, pickerel
scooting in fright as I crash into water
and with long strokes rhythmic as breathing
I arrive at the lake's dead center and twist
muscling through water down the clutch
of oily weeds, something flocking by
with its packed mosaic of scales
and I touch bottom where the ancient
silt is, fine as chalk dust,
then twisting in a somersault kick up
looking for the faint dusting of stars
overhead to break and scatter them
across the surface, to lie breath-
less and buoyant.

But now all shores look the same.
Down below a bubbling sound like
water in the throat and the bulk
of a submerged houseboat grunts
as it settles again in silt.
Sleep is, I think, a serum, a way
of defending ourselves from sleep,
that final sinking, that
treading on a half-rotten board
and breaking through.

# Afterwards, Her Monologue

What called me back when I leaned
my hand bent back against the window
so that glass could get at the wrist
and the cup full of blood leapt to out-
shoot the chiming fall of glass,
pink misting the air,
was the knock of a puzzled heart.
Dumb and faithful as the tide
I felt it panic, a stubborn fist's quick
clenching, floundering in fight,
in a labor all its own. Then,
knew it was no part of me
beating on and on
for its reason alone.

# Afterwards

What do we do now who loved you for your felicity
—you who traded for nothing—or what?

Frost thickens your car's exhaust
to the windfall scent of winesaps.
Swallows tip sunlight through the sugar maples.

You cherished these "gratuities," as you said,
leaving us with your awful forfeiture,
slack hands, mouths, lives.

23

# Pillage

*Now the year's down*
*to the last rich sediment of summer.*

The sad footpath back through dune grass.
Over-ripe grapes along the way
are fattened up for spoilage.

*What's tainted is also what's*
*done for in its ripe residue.*

The goat's loose in the garden
mauling tomatoes over the black peat moss.
He splits them back from their skins
to the red plush inside.

*All is softened booty's final plunder.*

Tonight, a stranger's smell
in the house, his
wet coughing.

*What's been feared for*
*now's up for good.*

# Sunday Afternoon Ice Fishing

*"There's a certain slant of light"*

The sky's leaden as ice.
Pickups roll over the lake
—mud-splattered miracles
bouncing on broken springs.
They make the ice rumble
all the way to shore
where trees poke up like sticks
through snow.

Wind has found its way
into this miserable shack.
It warps the flame
and the fire coughs
ashes over the snow.
It's putting itself out
sizzling ice. A snort
or two of vodka helps
and a few drops make
the flame leap up with hope.
Time is measured by cold:
how often the hole skims over
with ice, the falling level
of the bottle.

Down in the chapel dim light,
winter stunned,
a fish lips the bait.
I drag him unthrashing up.
It's the long slick length
of a pike, yellow and black
and speckled with pebble shine.

Though he's dying he's
the only brightly alive thing for miles.
I watch the freezing tail curl
slowly into a question mark, blood
color ice red as stained glass;
lug the weight of him home.

# Coming Back

Now when the wind shifts
you can hear the hiss
of traffic through trees. Nearby,
a tire has rolled up
against that elm. It leans
as if to match the tree's
slow growth of rings
against its own miles
spun around the rim.

And this was the pool
and the wavering arrowhead settled in sand,
its white flint, the weight of it,
strangeness of water
that fell from my fingers, cold
wonder of the one
who had chipped and notched it.

# Weltschmerz

*"E Pluribus Unum"*

The boy's sent down to the rubber boat to account
for his father's loose change where hundreds of coins
chatter and wink with each wave knock in the morning
     sun
and where by noon the aluminum lake's beaten flat
as hot coins smear his fingers green—their smell
of body grease, sweat, blood and rust smutch.

The tarnishing sun has stained lakewater to tea
as he hefts the sackful or ordered hours home.
Green light sickles at a cant through the trees.
Oily slick of pine needles under foot.
There's a sour of brass on the tongue, on the air.

Then how to restore to him the loon's apricot cry at night
when the lake each night will again mint
its ribbed signatures on the lake floor
and the world's imprest fall to his fingertips
in all forms of astonishing coinage.

# California Gardens

The spring morning's lush as a melon.
Last night's rain beads the grass.
Light green as the in-
side of an avocado fills the glade
and in the garden
trees blighted and bitten with smog
are letting their fruit drop.
The smooth lawn is rumpled
with hard, young-nippled oranges
tapped with spots of soft rot.
They dent the ground with round thumps,
a drum's slow roll call.
A wind puff brings a scent of sweet
suppuration like a twist of silk
across the lawn.

# Jogging the Lake

> *. . . ice*
> *Is also great*
> *And would suffice.*

I tell you these days it's strange
running over the snow-covered ice,
fat flakes coming down like downy
fall-out, thinking of the cold-
clobbered fish drifting any way
the mercury-heavy water moves them
as I run through a small town of ice
shanties, pieds-à-terre furnished with
one stool, a quart of vodka, each
with a parked pick up, a barking dog
inside. Now there's a bewildered cluster
of ducks whose heads swing on a hinge
as I go by. Their confusion is so
complete they've given up flying
along with swimming.
And the maniacs who all day still
drive over the lake like gorillas,
brake and slide side-
ways or spin pin-
wheeling out of control,
slopping gaudy gas on the ice
—even after they've hit soft spots, lake
springs, and their cars splinter through
and bubbling settle up
to headlights in the frozen mud
and send out a crazing of cracks.

At night you hear the muttering lake
—long booming rumbles. It's
the tightening cold mending faults.
And what of the icy white mountain north
of here, its stirring and grunting, its bulk
getting ready to heave itself south,
heftier, more towering than all of Manhattan?

# A Cluster of Plants around the TV

In the morning sun
one's blanched and slack,
its neighbor gone from *its* green hue
to a bristling and healthy yellow;
Another has a bruised and bloated purple
look. They no longer take
to water, shun and cower from sunlight.
Picking one up there's an almost audible snarl
as it shrinks from touch. Its pot struck
rings with a *thonk* as if filled with coins,
chrome washers, shiny screws, bolts.
One has lopped a vine brotherly
over the shoulders of the set.
Before the news comes on
—and make of this what you will—
they start to agitate, whisper
and rustle together, nervously waving their leaves
and seem to hump in their fubsy pots
hunkering closer.
With the late news they're atwitter
—an excitable hiss like angry bees.
They stretch and crane in their pots
getting their turgor up for Leno, then
collapse back spent and limp
with a long collective sigh.
At 3 a.m. they nod and flutter
soothed by the TV's snow,
its white sound and smug
from the scratch
of a vine outside wanting in.

# 3

## Unfabling

# Spring Snow At 9,000 Feet

I cut into an orange,
release its heavy sweetness to the sun.
Its tartness has a sting
like the thin air
that both kills and keeps alive.
The wind's cut keeps
the soft snow hard. Its hum
through snow pines
is a crushed green scent.
Underfoot you can hear
old snow melting, first
splash of spring.
Mountain shadow inches
black to white over the valley floor.
The orange rind curls in the cold
finding the source of its tropical heat.

Smoke from the coal furnace
laces snow with soot, its black smell
puzzling the clear air.
All afternoon her hands
puzzle over a Chopin étude
going from the white keys to the black.
When night comes taking the valley
a line of snow shine scales the walls,
black notes sounding through the house
like the mountain's shadow darkening snow outside,
hardening to the cold as old sugar might.

# The World's Shape

*For Clara and Bob*

## I.

Even your old car's fenders round-
ed as these foot hills.
We roll to a stop
near the river that's churning up icy mica.
An hour ago its water was a round
of snow above the timberline's lunar scree.
Now it rushes over watercress
pulling the oblong leaves, white flowers magnified,
unmelting under water.
Barefoot, we gather up handfuls.

In the evening where the river ponds out
birds flick over water picking off insects.
A swallow holds the cupped curve of its wing for a
       moment.
It's the same shape as your arched instep
and the new moon's crescent lies
on the water cut by the world's shape:
lip, eyelid or pared fingernail.
Watching water run under the brightening moon,
I think how the Queen saw through
the sophistry of flatness,
—how a curve already completes intent.

## II.

Swimming the hot springs in the pre-dawn cold
was like plunging back down past sleep:
hot pulse of green copper salt,
red oxide, sulphur held
in the blind underground now uncapped,
its mineral broth tasting like sea brine that
bubbled and brimmed over the caked pool
the Spaniards called *ojos*—eyes.

Clara floats nearby on the thick brew
and Bob, his beard frozen in a tined,
twisted shape looks like a demented Proteus.
Steam rising slabs pine boughs with ice,
each needle a threaded ice bead.
First light comes curving through all that space.
Quick spurt like a match high overhead,
pink spreading to orange
then red down the mountains
and the day coming round again
filling itself with light like no other.

# Where the Moving Circle's Center Is

Was that really how it was,

when you told me about the movie
making it seem real,
to have happened just that way?

The director, then, must have seen it all
right from the book,
when you told me about the wet mountains
and the young girl with long, loose hair,
their making love.

Was the author there when
as you told me snow fell at night,
winter closing the mountains for good?

Maybe he never saw these things
or if he did, do I have it right?

I mean the way I'm telling it now?

# the girl who went out stalking deer,

a shadow pliant as water
armed with a flashlight to lure
them closer,
to unfable them,
rumor them real,

out of the upland meadow
where the brook slows and pools,
a small shelf of the mountain,
a green step,

where they come at night
to the glade
luminous in ground fog.

The flashlight's strange charm—
not foxfire,
the phosphorescent glow
from an old stump—it

halts them in a frieze.
She's stopped them now
with a fistful of light,
moon chip, a burning hand,
or shine gathered from distant
window panes.

Everything in that clear-
ing listens hard.
Whatever breathes has stopped:
the breath of birds, brook water hold-
ing to its pools

before they're gone:
a champagne swirl,
hooves and antlers in a brindled blur
leaving in the glade
ripped gauze of ground fog.

The long beam of the flashlight
goes out like a star fading
down in a well as if what the world
wants to confide is a dream
that slips off,
that breaks apart like water.

# Night Swimming

All day hearing the lake's
strange music,
so at night, sly as an eel,
I slip into the lake
wrapped in nothing but water;
pass over the cold pulse of springs
where the moon's made a wavering lick
and head for the racket of lights
where slurred chatter
of talk and laughter splashes
lavender over the lake.

Under the dock I see
through the lighted slats:
small tread of a sneaker, trim
of lacy underwear. A dribble of gin
falls on my shoulder,
her voice over the lake, shoes
treading the wobbling dock.
I slide away going deep
where something live
swirls up sediment,
through the silky weeds,
out to lake center
to lie supine, lungs
bringing air back into the body.

Then the Chicago train
strains around the lake curve:
its concussion of air bucks
over the water lapping
against this body that rests
half-submerged in animalculae,
—this foreign flesh that must have known
the ooze down below,
that now glows a pale green;
the body's tiny lights,
hair like cilia; strange
how the knock of a human heart
must sound through water.

The lake crumples,
closes behind me as I climb out.
A spell of dizziness from the tilting lawn.
I fling off water to starlight
—circles of bright beads,
a casting off of scales.

Coarseness of concrete underfoot
and the railing's live wood to the touch;
into this strangely changed room
where the shine of light bulbs falls
on a gaudy sheen of magazines,
the Bakelite telephone
and the TV's fat eye
seems to stare forever into itself.

# I.  Passing Time on the Mainland

### Summer Solstice: 21 June '97

This hand-carved oar
chocked by ocean rock, lodged in limestone;
knocked down by sea spray, hands sliced by reef rock
and running with blood, I had to see how hands
shaped a tree limb. I wrested it out
as if it were a sword; saw how first it was chipped
and scalloped like waxing and waning moons along the
     pole,
then made to flair out flat at the end
and topped by a small platform fit for a palm,
how time had made notches from
a gripping curl of fingers at gunnel length.

Out there beyond sight an island,
its cobbled walkways under notched corbel arches,
and where—when the sun today had been made to fit
its perfect square-shine through the temple door—
hands on my smashed wrist watch pointed no where.

## II.  Passing Time: What To Do on the Island

It's enough to wake any time from the cathedral bell:
three centuries old, a heavy, sage sound;
And at noon's hot stasis, to watch the pulse pump
along the ancient iguana's suède throat.

It's enough to hear not just at night
the seep and drip of water ticking everywhere
through underground grottoes of limestone shells
tiny as fingernails
before going out to sea

—enough to know that here
where reckoning of the dead is kept

# Letter from Isla de Cozumel, Quintana Roo, México

In a veranda cunningly cross-woven
with palm fronds I slowly gather up
my drowsy wits having woken at 4 a.m.
to a tantrum of lashed palm
and banana trees and just
as suddenly stopped to a few drops
stepping lightly down
a terrace of broad leaves.
Then the moon reappeared
putting down its blue enamel
so the lawn's now alive,
leaping with an ornate fret work of leaf shadow.
The disco in town pumps out
a thudding bass beat feathering
runs of ripples over hotel pools,
then from inland a strange
counterpoint:
purple chorus of roosters
descanting from jungle ranches.
Out on the Boulevard's slick
cobbles a car's chattering slobber
of rubber tires are grabbing
for purchase like a drawn out lilt
of a question being asked,
but instead of a crash there's a crunch
of car doors, spit and click

of Mayan cursing, crazed laughter, the shot
then splintered splash of broken bottles.
The disco thump rocks to a stop.
Racket dies out over the surf.
A black cat unbecomes a shadow
dragging a severed goat's head
backwards across the lawn.
This, then, gringos, is the moment which marks
that day is about to begin.
With the first touch of sun
this island circled by a ring
of sand finer than cocaine
and mounted in jade
seems to rise up sluicing sea water,
steaming from out of the ocean again.

# Translating Lourdes

Lourdes at work in the bank,
a pavilion of black marble:
phone at each ear,
another ringing at her desk.
Voices come mixed with water,
she says, and paper money muttering.
She's one generation from
a stick shack in the jungle.

Tonight when the power goes off
like a slammed door all
over the island her array
of candles lights up the circus-
colored room like a festive shrine.
Her eyes in candlelight go
from bright black to cinnamon
and her small hands weave the air
quick as swallows as if *they'd*
tracked down the words,
person, tense,
ordered and knotted them all
together into perfect English.

I wake at 3 a.m. when the lights leap
on again. The half-translated
New York Times is a blizzard
of loose pages around the bed.
I hear her mutter scraps of Mayan
in her sleep. She still
grips my hand. Over what precarious bridge
does she want to be led? Outside,
a tropical moon large and round
as a manhole cover's spiked
on a palm tree
and all around us phosphorescent
wetlight rings up on shore like snow
from hundreds of TVs left on all night.

*Cozumel was originally called
"Ah Cuzamil Peten,"
Land of the Swallows,
by the Maya.*

# Off Shore Suite

### I. Descent

Seen from the beach a cruise ship hangs
free of its own weight buoyed
on what seems nothing but pure air,
its shadow bolted to the sea's floor.

Swimming through the surf's milk froth,
out to where you descend
into a village of coral
through water tinted apple-green,
sun on the honey floor
lighting up orange shells,
sea stones and a dash of small fish
silvering down like summer rain
and further out where lettuce-colored water
deepens to a thicker blue so looking up's
a view of sky matched
and lacquered over sky—this watery Eden!

But always on your back,
heft of thick tonnage, swaying weight
of water; strange tickings from the sea floor,
ancient lurch of sand, pebble knock,
unearthly pingings and the salt slick body more,
then more unbalanced in the ocean's monstrous dance,
its urge to let earth's air in,
mix and bubble in the blood.

## II. Shark

I sit sunpinked and shaken, propped in a plastic beach
    chair
near a litter of pink flippers, rubber mask.
The equatorial sun stuns the water clear down
so as to seem there's no water there at all,
where I'd poked at the reef's clutter, its scree
of sand dollars, shells; puny splashes in the heat-
quiet noon when the knock of a discarded conch
on a sea rock stopped him, a shadow blackening the
    cream
and coral floor—sleek packet of grey, sheathed
like shell casing, but a blood veined thing,
mouth ragged as a ripped tin can. A flattened eye
tilted in its socket, then
a twist of muscle made him no longer where he was,
mere displacement of lighter matter.
Then this biped body, its blood still
bounding through a maze of veins,
struggling to make action and thought the same—the
    jump
the moment before the jump the same.

### III.  Hurricane Watch

An afternoon of strange light,
either too bright or dark.
The ocean's flat as a football field
but shells below tell something about
the way the tonnage of water's moving.

Strange colors contesting over the ocean's face,
bottle-green given over to black.
There's an old memento on the water's edge
—an overturned bulldozer the ocean's
working to make its own.

Waves limp then fall slack.
Now a yellow light's shrinking the pupil's eye.
Birds are gone from where now there's no breath
in the taut thrumming of the upper air.

# Vigilando: Staying Up All Night

*After Vallejo*

To be the poem and not have to write it.
Darkness won't stop every night
covering the island, like a scarf of mourning,
like a museum that's locked up until morning.
Now the young whores are waking up in the brothel.
Why should day exist for them
when every night's carnival?

Who wants to be walking around dead
and not know of it?;
the insolence of the light house beam
trying to temper the ocean.
There's Diego dead drunk again
in the plaza and why not?
Aren't these letters already ghosting out?

Morning's first blood colors the ocean.
Now Esperanza and Epifania are safe
as angels locked in the bordello.
Don Diego is finding his way home. Soon
they'll open the museum which is what each day is
and bodies made up out of air and light and water
will rise up again all over the island.

*Cozumel*

51

# 4

## Duplicate moon

# Sun after Three Days of Rain

*. . . all men are Noah's sons.*  Richard Wilbur

Suddenly all the small hammerings stop, dead
silence after a racket of carpentry.
The driven nails, silver rivets of rain
must have kept the whole earth together from
crumbling apart; or was it the drunk-
en neighbors all around us building an ark
knowing something we didn't about the small lakes
spreading over the lawn, making a moat
of the driveway while we were carried out
again and again on the tides of this bed
as if to find in the rain its original wetness
even as it could have come up to test
its weight against the window
for all we knew?
Then in a burst of white birdsong
through sodden silence we came out chaste-
ned and blinking under the earth
baking sun, survivors into a world
made all over again in green.

# Dispairities

### I. Vive l'égalité

He scowls at the trespassing snow
marcelled across his bevelled lawn
which just overnight has messed up
the neighborhood, unrectangulating block,
plot and brick, plumping sill
and shutter, each roof's
voluptuous swell;
even the rigid grid
of wire-covered gutters
is worked into feminine filigree,

But then sees down the street
how like sets of mail order dentures
his house rightfully fits the look
of his neighbors,
sets off to work with a whistle.

## II.

Your red sports car embossed with chrome.
Bright as a jelly bean it flaunts even more
its foreign élan deep into these woods
parked there on the mossy floor.

Evening and light's the odor of kerosene.
Look—an invading raccoon steps over
plastic bowls on the kitchen's plastic counter top—
how burnished his brindled coat is

even with the night's spilled ink
spreading through the woods
blotting out each tree's own
font of leaf and twig there is

the flowing signature of your hair,
print of fingertips, a bite's imprimatur,
your furred and pear-halved sex,
    and knowing this is I because this is you.

# Traveling with One Suitcase

*For T.*

A shower of coins—yellow leaves—spins
behind us. We've left the old forest,
come out to what's called the lake effect
with its strange orange and cinnamon flowers,
the land spongy, wet-green.

Now October light like your yellow perfume
comes through the car's canvas roof,
the road getting blonder approaching
the lake's glassy light.

And tonight the moon's whole barrel,
a tumble of jackpot dimes,
half dollars all over the lake.
What abundance, abandon
at the tipped-over end of summer.

# Measures

Always on this island there's
the measured thump of surf
regular as breathing, where
this morning going for water
we saw how the well's surface felt
rippling over and over with each roll
of a wave coming to shore and at night
when the sweep of the lighthouse beam
kept coming and going through rooms
like the breathings of a gigantic ghost
and later when the kerosene lamp pulsed
its beat across the shuddering bed,
we found ourselves changed, taken
again and again by such measures
matching each other breath for breath,
changing just as the same shore does
each morning: the reinvention of its
beach, the sea-floor re-ribbed again.

# Absences: Negative Space

Bed sheets are tangled,
limber as rope. Outside,
a weave of sun and wind spills
through trees, makes what I think's
her shadow jump across the window;
or a tree limb that's wind-rubbed scrapes
on the gutter like the scuff of her foot
on the porch. A nervous wind keeps
trying the door, slight gauze of her scent
floats in the air—all of these making of her
both less and more than she is.

At noon, wind distracts the lake.
The boat's reflection wobbles on the water.
It's not the wind's sound. We know
the wind by a drawnout sigh of leaves.
With her gone something else
becomes of her: what can't be seen
or touched. The oak casts off
its tossing mass of shadow.

Now that she's here right
before the sun goes down
when the lake is slick
and the boat's reflection only seems
truer than the boat itself,
I want to make her give her shadow up,
know the very breath of her,
get back her deepest scent.
But watery lights keep rising
like echoes re-echoing through the room,
reflections only borrowed for a moment
from the darkening lake.

## Poem Begun on the Back of an Envelope Returned & Stamped: *Moved—Left No Forwarding Address*

The year's frozen into silence
but for the sound
of a shingle's slack
flapping in the wind.
The sunflower's eye is tattered beyond measure
of the sun's dim disc,
lopped at the neck lolling,
bantered by its own boney applause
when the wind clatters through the glade.

In the root cellar eyes
of potatoes grope in dimness.
Onions are wrapped in sepia
and a tumble of sheenless apples lay shriveled.
The smell of earth still hounds them all
—sullen to have come to this.

The sun going down takes with it all
color.
Like an eye its round of light blinks once
on the lake's ice,
dulls
and is thumbed closed.

# Complaint

### I.

Another quarrel and the August heat drive
her from our bed, out to the dock, to any
curl of breeze, to bathe awhile
in the tea-warm lake, to lie
down in the limp rubber boat
and fall asleep,
drift the night around its augured stake
in what since spring
our excited mingled breathing kept afloat.

### II.

Why do I weary the night and the rain
invoking all the elements once more,
berating her when all I need
is to open the door and let it go.
It must be the way the wind is
on the lake tonight,
the inquiring rain,
how candles flared along the bathtub's rim,
wind jostling the house
so that water lapped your leg,
steam pearling your skin,
damp hair, green eyes, *that* look
making the earth itself still
seem untrustworthy dropping through space.

# Stored Honey

*For JCL—mother, apiarian(1907-1997)*

Through cellardust, lace-
work of spiderwebs, these fat
gold nests, hostages to summer,
seem to give off a hum.
In the gloom there's a glow
of amber light they generate themselves,
the final harvest—caught and caged—
of August's poured yellow heat,
or chestnut colored, crushed
from September's press of goldenrod.

Its heft like a live weight
in my hand upstairs to where
frost has scratched its
puzzle of glyphs across the window pane.
White combs of snow are rising
in the fields, the wind
forcing its way through
the chimney's humming flue.
Though honey comes heavy from the jar
as if still stunned from the weight
of summer's ransomed sun,
it gathers to itself
all of winter's available light.

# Returning

I suck in the hot night,
heavy as whisky neat, humid
as hay rotting in the loft.
From the garden over-ripe
with softened tomatoes and pears
groundfog lifts its scent of spilled wine.
I enter the house:
each step's a wooden boom
through emptied rooms.
I stop at the stairs when a click
like a spark comes from the cupboard
—a field mouse nudging the left-over teacup
and then from upstairs: a child's cough, a
dreamcry and a noise knots in my throat.
I climb the stairs from old habit, find
the right door and walk in: moonlight's
curdled on a pile of newspapers
from leftover packing
and the whole bedroom wall
vibrates with the click and crawl
of hundreds of bees humming
in anger—a yellow pelt
moving in moonlight—new hosts
freshly hived in the house.

# Traces: Some Old Photographs Recovered

*You who are free,*
*Rescue the dead.*

David Ignatow


## Jacob's Model T

This Jake's got X-ed out, cartoon eyes,
his blacksmith arm hooked on the car's roof.
And who's that woman behind in a swirl
of white clothes who has smeared herself from the scene?
More raw light was let in then
through the skinny trees along the shore
so the lake further behind's
like a flat aluminum lid.
Jake's black Ford shines like a wet plum, but


## On the North Shore

Too much light's been leeched from this.
Nameless, they ghost out even more
from the moment: her head's cocked
as if listening for what it was
that splashed into the lake,
but then we see in one dim corner a child's
small shape tottering with its first
ungainly gait over the lawn,
and the woman in white?
is raising her arms to her legacy, like

64

## Sarah on Belle

Sidesaddle, frightened, trying to hold up
a string of bass and pike. Belle won't stand
for the stink. Her back's humped up
ready to buck. Jake has her snubbed down tight
by the reins and with one hand
clamps her breathing shut
where there's no bone along the nose.
Was he the one who led the mare out
over the ice, weighted,
then killed her, whose wired memento mori bones just
last week came to light on shore? near

## Benson's Ice House

A place without windows, an archive
and a heaped-up pile of sawdust that
tries to preserve through another summer
melting away what happened in the lake through the
        years.
It must be cool as a crypt inside,
the great monoliths of ice marbled with oxides.
Through their blue translucence
will be teeth chips, hair,
mineral traces of our lives
with rows and rows of hollow breath beads
scored like a rising run of notes or voices,
sustaining as the hope of water is
into its other state.

# Right Now

*Now is the time that face should form another;*
*Whose fresh repair if now thou not renewst,*
*Thou dost beguile the world, unbless some mother.*
Shakespeare, sonnet III

*For C.L. & L.L.*

By the lake and with her first handful of steps,
this first ungainly but upright gait,
her daughter has shocked herself
as if she'd stumbled into perfect speech.
Her mother has her arms out now and waits.
It's as if the rising moon has stopped
for awhile and through the half-light
there's a sound of an oar cracked
down on the dock from across the lake
and someone saying *wait,*
the splash of an anchor, a jostle
like an earth tap and the small march
of waves across the water to where

The child's still ambling over the lawn,
her face a puzzle of frowns.
Fists like snails clench then un-
clench with her lurching gait
which will walk her out far from this moment.
But for now there's no husband, father, lover.
A duplicate moon's just
beginning to wander over the water.

# Epithalamium for my Daughter

*We need the landscape to repeat us.*
W. D. Snodgrass

Mountain kid, our small water sprite,
conceived while we slept
while above the timberline
sunlight still shone inside the glacier,
surely we are made and known
by where it is we first breathe
the world in.
The morning your lungs caught
and held their own first breath
—August's scent of cedar and hot pine pitch—
came mixed with the miracle of water,
came cold and crushed from under the glacier
leaping its talisman coins of sunlight
down Copper Ridge Creek.

Water like any miracle
is known by what it makes happen:
how I looked out that August morning
—the whole mountain green again
circled by its bracelets of water,
how you came re-greening our lives,
braiding our lives together,

And now you're back where you took that first breath,
to braid your life together with another,
to breathe your lives into each other
which is also the earth's breath
where water first
gathers again under the glacier
flashing down into this valley
bright as mountain mica,
where each bead is your own
small, incipient sun.

*Steamboat Springs, Colorado*
*August, 1994*

# Tools

The curious dormant nature of tools
becoming more than themselves in their quick
and singular way of performing:
Snowshoes making the body's weight a lie
over twenty foot drifts—web-footed
again I get to the river
where the fishing rod asleep in its limber
length jumps suddenly alive when the fish's strike
leaps right into my hands.

Idle on the back porch the shovel's
angle is to the point in its way
of getting under the surface. Through use
its handle is turning to harder wood
from layers of petrified sweat
and the bridle hangs stiff on a nail
saving the shape of the mare's head,
remembering a mouth.

Red and silver rainbow trout freeze
on the snow as the sun goes down and the hot-
tempered ax head caught in the tightening grip
of the cold finally gets its crack
at a tree limb. Later the castiron woodstove
gathers to itself all the heat it can handle.
Smoke rises up to the cold night's crisp stars,
impalpable almost as words
but which in their right use still have their way
of getting us through to the world
alive for a moment.

Douglas Lawder has received grants from the National Endowment for the Arts, the Danforth Foundation, Michigan Council for the Arts, and the Colorado Council on the Arts. His work has appeared in *The Nation, Poetry (Chicago), Poetry Northwest, The Seventies,* and *The Virginia Quarterly Review.* His first book *Trolling* was published by Little, Brown & Co. He lives in Colorado and in Cozumel, Mexico.